Let's Say

You are Bullshit

Swear Word Coloring Book

By

S.B. Nozaz

MOTHER

FUCKER

ASS

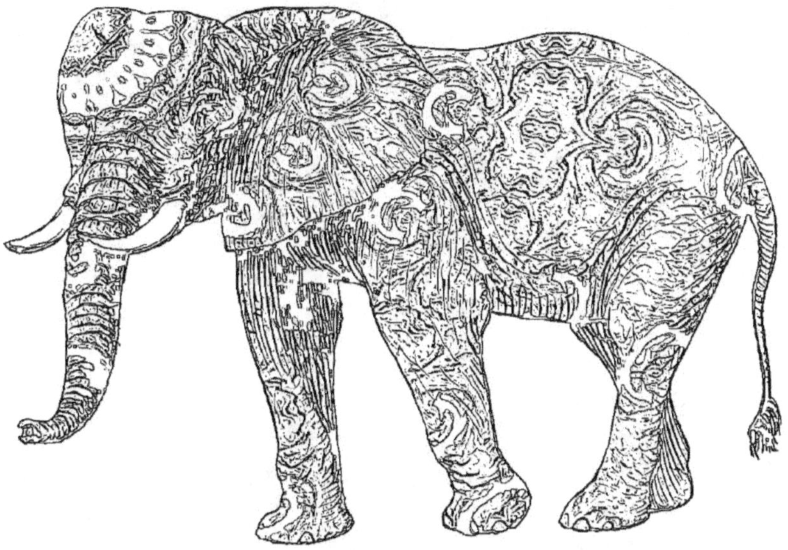

MORON

SICKO

WHAT THE

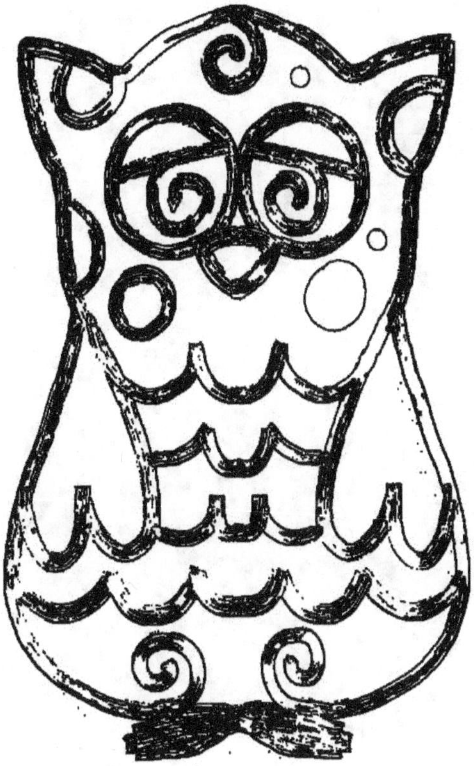

HELL

GET THE

FUCK OUT

Note

www.ingramcontent.com/pod-product-compliance
Lightning Source LLC
Chambersburg PA
CBHW080325290526
45793CB00006B/1208